THIS WALKER BOOK BELONGS TO:

LISA

By the SEA

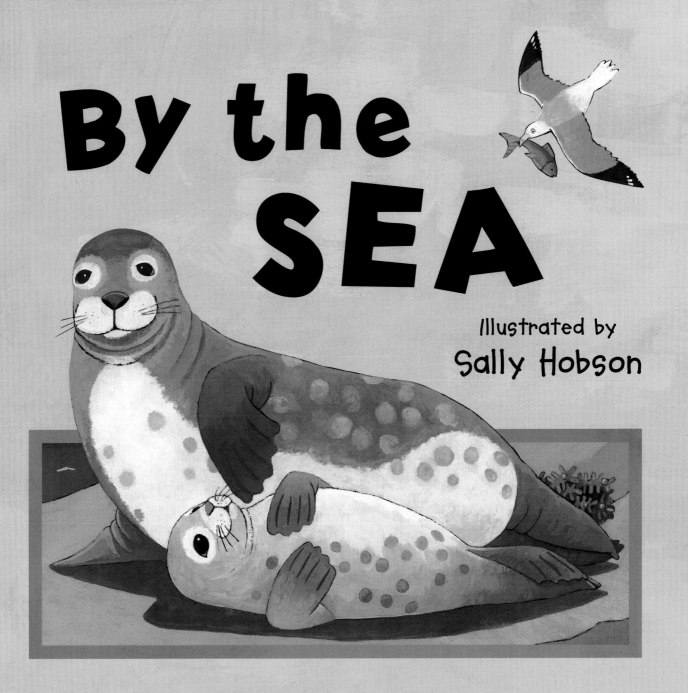

Illustrated by
Sally Hobson

WALKER BOOKS
AND SUBSIDIARIES
LONDON • BOSTON • SYDNEY

Whose
blue
boat
is this?

scuttle
scuttle

Whose
sharp
claws
are these?

aaarf
aaarf

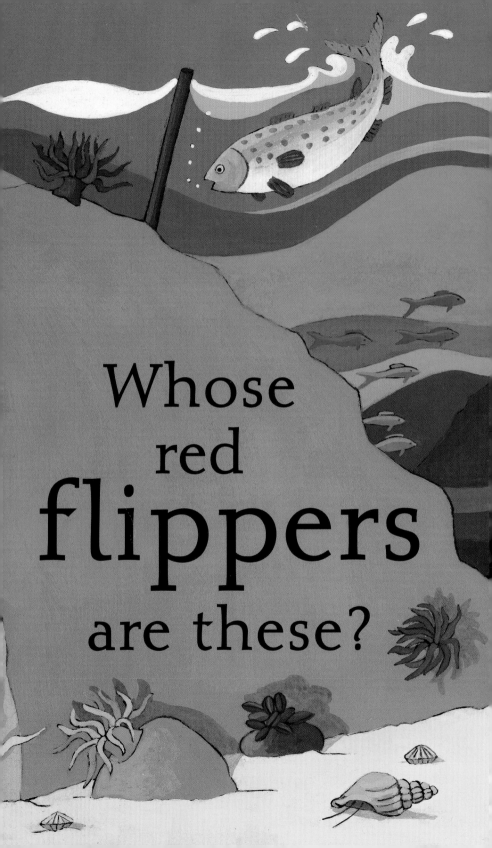

Whose
red
flippers
are these?

My flippers help
me to move quickly
when I go swimming.

keeeow
keeeow

Whose long **wing** is this?

My long wings
help me to glide slowly
over the sea looking
for food.

creep
creep

Whose orange **arms** are these?

I have suckers
on my knobbly
arms for clinging
on to rocks.

Here we are, by the sea.
Can you find the fisherman, the starfish,
the snorkeler, the seagull, the crab
and the seal?

First published 2000 by Walker Books Ltd
87 Vauxhall Walk, London SE11 5HJ

This edition published 2001

2 4 6 8 10 9 7 5 3 1

Series concept and design by Louise Jackson

Words by Paul Harrison and Louise Jackson

Wildlife consultant: Martin Jenkins

This book has been typeset in Calligrahic

Printed in China

British Library Cataloguing in Publication Data:
a catalogue record for this book
is available from the British Library

ISBN 0-7445-7748-9

Walker Flip-flap Facts

ISBN 0-7445-7748-9 (pb)

ISBN 0-7445-7749-7 (pb)

ISBN 0-7445-7750-0 (pb)

ISBN 0-7445-7751-9 (pb)

Collect them all!